HAZARDOUS

HABITATS

AND

ENGANDERED

ANIMALS

WELBECK

THIS IS A WELBECK CHILDREN'S BOOK

Published in 2021 by Welbeck Children's Books
An imprint of Welbeck Children's Limited, part of
Welbeck Publishing Group
20 Mortimer Street, London W1T 3JW

ISBN: 978-1-78312-652-1

Printed in Dongguan, China

10 9 8 7 6 5 4 3 2 1

Commissioning Editor: Bryony Davies
Design Manager: Emily Clarke
Editor: Elly Dowsett
Art Editor: Sam James
Designers: Jake da'Costa and
Intrepid Books LTD.
Picture Researcher: Paul Langan
Production: Nicola Davey

FSC
www.fsc.org
MIX
Paper from
responsible sources
FSC® C144853

The publishers would like to thank the following sources for
their kind permission to reproduce the pictures and footage
in this book. The numbers listed below give the page on which
they appear in the book. (T=top, B=bottom, L=left, R=right,
C=center)

ALAMY: /WaterFrame: 14-15

GETTY IMAGES: /Martin Bureau/AFP: 53L

NATURE PICTURE LIBRARY: /Mark Bowler: 23BL; /Mark
Carwardine: 25B, 27B; /Jordi Chias: 43TR; /Tui De Roy: 16T,
51TL; /Leo & Mandy Dickinson: 56BL; /Gerry Ellis: 25T; /David
Fleetham: 48BR; /Jurgen Freund: 46L; /Dr Axel Gebauer:
57BR; /Edwin Giesbers: 57TC; /Mitsuaki Iwago: 50-51; /
Steven Kazlowski: 58; /Valeriy Maleev: 57TR; /Thomas
Marent: 4C, 18-19; /Luiz Claudio Marigo: 37TL; /Claus Meyer:
22-23; /Hiroya Minakuchi: 23BCR; /Fred Olivier: 5C, 54-55; /
Pete Oxford: 50B, 51TC; /Mike Parry: 47BL; /TJ Rich: 4T, 6-7; /
Kevin Schafer: 16C; /Philip Stephen: 48L; /Paul D Stewart:
51TR; /Wim van der Heever: 56-57; /Staffan Widstrand: 27T; /
Tony Wu: 7C

SCIENCE PHOTO LIBRARY: /Dr Morley Read: 8-9

SHUTTERSTOCK: /AS Inc: 1, 2-3; /AlinaMD: 52BR; /Allexxandar:
48-49; /Arcady: 61BR; /Andrey Armyagov: 5T, 40-41; /
ArnuphapY: 40B; /Austral Int: 38BR; /Beer1024: 29R; /
Bildagentur Zoonar GmbH: 10BL; /biletskiyevgeniy.com: 35R; /
Brichuas: 58L; /Rich Carey: 14BR, 21BL, 21BR, 52-53; /Ramon
Carretero: 42BC; /Cat Act Art: 10R; /Chainfoto24: 45TR; /
Cherstva: 51B (person); /DJTaylor: 39TR; /Damsea: 44-45; /
Danm12: 5B, 60-61; /Chase Dekker: 8TL; /Marcos del Mazo
Valentin: 45B; /DigitalNatureScotland: 19C; /eAlisa: 57TL; /
David Evison: 21TR; /Peter Fodor: 33BR; /Svetlana Foote:
21BCR; /Stanislav Fosenbauer: 8TR; /Funkyplayer: 30BL; /
Juan Gaertner: 8BR; /Giedriius: 16B; /GizmoPhoto: 16TC; /
Tom Goaz: 8BL; /Leonardo Gonzalez: 49BR; /Handoko
Ramawidjaya Bumi: 21TC; /Kerry Hargrove: 31TR; /Mark
Higgins: 21TL; /Paul Michael Hughes: 52R; /Hung Chung Chih:
23BR, 26-27; /Hunthomas: 13TR; /Ian 2010: 17T; /Ink Drop:
61TR; /Javarman: 24B; /Kashurka: 60BL; /Kazoka: 17B; /
Erika Kirkpatrick: 37R; /Lunamarina: 42BR; /Makhh: 24-25; /
Maggy Meyer: 4B, 30-31, 35TL, 35TCL; /Joe Morris 917:
42-43; /Mr.anaked: 43L; /Oleksandra Naumenko: 53TR; /
Nerthuz: 17TC; /Shin Okamoto: 14L; /Vlasto Opatovsky: 32-33;
/Ostill is Franck Camhi: 23BCL; /Pio3: 22B, 34B; /Pking4th:
51B (camera); /Stu Porter: 35TR; /Anton Prohorov: 51B (bin);
/Ondrej Prosicky: 16BC, 36-37, 37BL; /Pyty: 15T; /Stephen
William Robinson: 10-11; /Longchalerm Rungruang: 28-29; /
Roman Samokhin: 17BC; /Sedin: 43TL; /Singkham: 29L; /
Smileus: 4-5, 38-39; /Joseph Sohm: 28BR; /Donny Sophandi:
21BCL; /Studio Kiwi: 53TL; /Super Prin: 17C; /Andrew Sutton:
42BL; /Zoltan Tarlacz: 32BR; /Tarpan: 59T; /Anna Timoshenko:
16-17; /Travelgram2019 35TCR; /Ueuaphoto: 54B; /Sergey
Uryadnikov: 20-21, 34-35; /V_E: 46-47; /Vaalaa: 39TL; /
Wanprae.O: 23T; /Wavebreakmedia: 38BL

HAZARDOUS HABITATS AND ENGANDERED ANIMALS

Written by Camilla de la Bédoyère

WELBECK

CONTENTS

HOME SWEET HOME

Think about your home. It's the place you and your family feel safe. It has the basic things you need, like a cozy bed, food, water, and shelter from the weather. An animal's home is called a habitat, and it's just as important to them as your home is to you. When we damage habitats, the animals and plants that live in them may die. We haven't cared enough about the harm we've been doing, but things are changing.

FACT
At least one-fourth of all mammals are at risk of extinction. The number of endangered species will keep going up—unless we act now.

ANIMALS IN DANGER

When an entire type, or species, of animal struggles to survive, it's described as "endangered." That means it's at risk of extinction—dying out forever. One reason why more than 28,000 species of living things are endangered is because we have damaged their habitats.

ANIMAL HABITATS

A habitat can be as small as the crack between two pebbles or as large as an ocean. Animals and plants have evolved to suit their habitats, but many can live in more than one habitat or even build their own homes.

HOME MAKERS

Beaver

Beavers use branches to dam the flow of a river. This creates a deep pond, where they build a home called a lodge.

Termites

Termites are insects that build their homes from mud. Millions of termites can live in a single mound.

Clown fish

Clown fish live among the tentacles of a sea anemone. They're the only fish that isn't harmed by the sting of the tentacles.

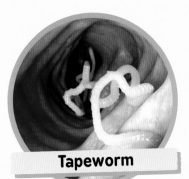

Tapeworm

Parasites live in or on other animals. Tapeworms live in the intestines and feed on their host's food as it passes through.

These tadpoles will grow into harlequin poison frogs. They hatched out of eggs laid in a tiny water reservoir on an aerial rain forest plant. As tadpoles, they swim and breathe in the water. Once they're frogs, with legs and lungs, they'll leave their first home.

OUR CROWDED WORLD

A hundred years ago, the world's population was around 2 billion people. Today there are more than 7.7 billion of us, and we all need water, food, and places to live. Humans have pushed animals out of their natural habitats by creating farms, mines, and cities.

INDUSTRIAL DAMAGE

FARMING

More than one-third of Earth's land is now used for farming. The chicken was probably the first animal to be farmed, about 10,000 years ago. Chickens are descended from the red jungle fowl, which lives in the forests of Asia. Today there are more than 20 billion chickens, but most are kept in cages.

MINING

Humans mine fossil fuels, metals, and minerals. This can destroy habitats and cause pollution. Cell phones contain mined materials including gold, silver, platinum, coltan, and aluminum oxide. Some of these are mined in the forests of the Democratic Republic of Congo, where gorillas once lived.

Thankfully, some species have been able to adapt to human activity. House sparrows nest in cities around the world. There are at least 500 million, but their numbers have fallen in recent years. Pollution and farming chemicals could be the cause.

TOTALLY TRUE - OR - FOOLISHLY FALSE?

A. Around the world, an area of forest equivalent to 36 football fields is destroyed every minute.

B. Palm oil plantations are habitats for 193 species of animals.

C. You should upgrade your cell phone every year.

Find the answers at the back of the book.

CLIMATE CHANGE

During Earth's 4.5 billion years, its climate has changed many times. It's been much hotter, colder, drier, and wetter than today. Most climate change is natural, but now our climate is being changed by human behavior—with devastating consequences.

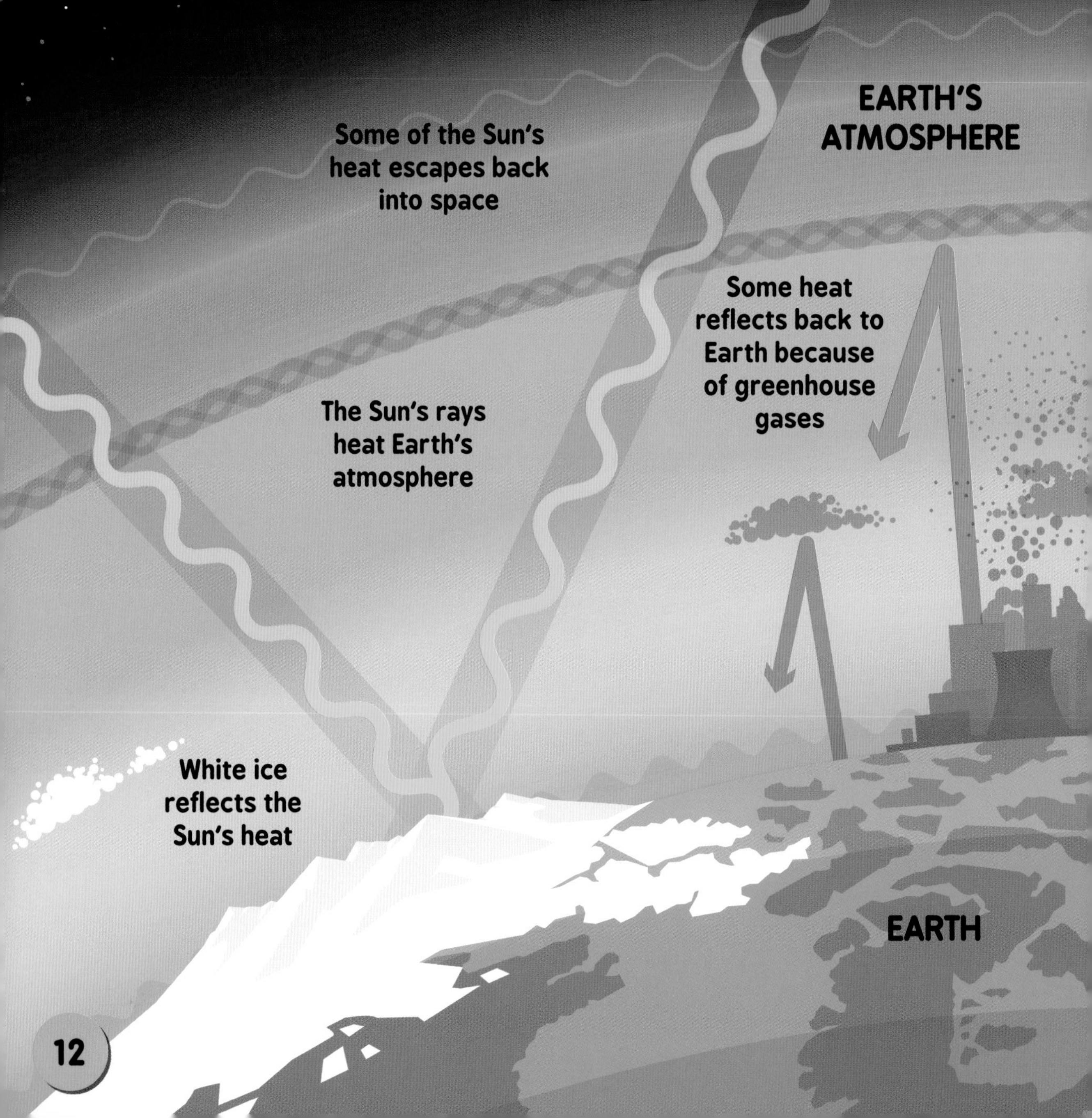

Some of the Sun's heat escapes back into space

EARTH'S ATMOSPHERE

Some heat reflects back to Earth because of greenhouse gases

The Sun's rays heat Earth's atmosphere

White ice reflects the Sun's heat

EARTH

SUN

GLOBAL WARMING
Fossil fuels are sources of energy like coal and natural gas. They were formed from animals and plants long ago. Like all living things, they contain carbon. When we burn fossil fuels for energy, the carbon combines with the air to make a gas called carbon dioxide, which is released into our atmosphere.

Layers of greenhouse gases

Burning fossil fuels release greenhouse gases into the atmosphere

THE GREENHOUSE EFFECT
Greenhouse gases such as carbon dioxide and methane work like a blanket that traps the Sun's energy close to Earth, warming up the atmosphere. This is called the greenhouse effect.

POLLUTION

Pollution is any harmful substance that enters the environment. It can affect the land, air, and water, turning these habitats into toxic places to live. Most air pollution is invisible, including carbon dioxide, which is released by burning fossil fuels.

WATER POLLUTION

Sewage (from humans and farm animals) and chemicals from factories and farms often find their way into oceans and fresh water. This turns them into hazardous habitats.

Mercury is a deadly metal that's released by burning coal and mining metal. It gets into the bodies of fish, dolphins, and small whales, and also the people who eat them.

More than 8 million pieces of plastic end up in the oceans every day. Plastic is now found on every beach, at the bottom of the sea, and even in Arctic ice.

ACID RAIN

Burning fossil fuels releases sulfur dioxide and nitrogen oxides. These gases react with water in the atmosphere to make acids. This toxic liquid is called acid rain, and it can wipe out forests. This happened in the "Black Triangle" in Central Europe, but the forest is now recovering after filters were added to power plants.

FACT
Cars release harmful particulates as well as carbon dioxide. And there are more particulates inside a car than outside it— a good reason to walk or bike!

Light pollution from electric lights can be harmful. When turtles hatch from their eggs on beaches, they use moonlight to guide them to the ocean. If they see artificial lights, they head inland and never make it to the water.

THE GREAT DYING

Five times in its history, Earth has seen more than three-fourths of its species wiped out. These periods are called mass extinction events (MEEs). Many scientists predict that we're entering the sixth MEE—and it's caused by humans.

EXTINCTION GUIDE

Scientists use five terms—ranging from extinct to vulnerable—to explain how close a species is to dying out forever.

 **EXTINCT:** No members of this species are left alive.

Floreana giant tortoise

 **EXTINCT IN THE WILD:** This species only survives in captivity, such as in zoos or wildlife parks.

Scimitar-horned oryx

 CRITICALLY ENDANGERED: This species faces an extremely high risk of extinction in the wild.

Pygmy raccoon

 **ENDANGERED:** This species faces a very high risk of extinction in the wild.

Tiger

 **VULNERABLE:** This species faces a high risk of extinction in the wild.

Southern rockhopper penguin

ENDANGERED SPECIES

Since 1964, the IUCN Red List (the International Union of Conservation of Nature's Red List of Threatened Species) has been collecting information about animals and plants. It shows that 28,000 species are at risk, including . . .

33%
of reef corals

30%
of sharks and rays

14%
of birds

25%
of mammals

40%
of amphibians

FOREST HABITATS

A single oak tree can be a habitat for hundreds of species of insects, so imagine how many animal homes exist in an entire forest! No one has counted all the world's trees, but there could be as many as three trillion—that's 3,000,000,000,000—and most grow in forests and woods.

TROPICAL FORESTS

Tropical forests grow where it's mostly hot, such as in the Amazon basin—the home of the spider monkey. Plenty of heat and rain create the perfect conditions for rain forests. Dry tropical forests grow where rainy seasons follow long, dry periods. Cloud forests grow on mountains, where it's colder and trees are often shrouded in dense cloud.

TEMPERATE FORESTS

Temperate forests grow in places that experience seasons with rain, warmth, and sunshine, such as in Europe, where the red squirrel lives. Deciduous trees cope with the cold by losing their leaves in order to rest and conserve energy through the winter months.

RAIN FORESTS

The rain forests of Sumatra and Borneo are diverse habitats. They're the only places where orangutans, tigers, rhinos, and elephants live in the wild together. However, humans are making these habitats hazardous.

WHERE IN THE
WORLD?

BORNEO

SUMATRA

The Bornean orangutan lives almost entirely in the rain forest treetops. Every night, it builds itself a bed from leafy branches. There are only about 104,700 Bornean orangutans left.

AWESOME ANIMALS AT RISK

These are just three of the many rain forest creatures under threat:

Sumatran tiger

Sumatran rhinoceros

Borneo pygmy elephant

RAIN FOREST THREATS

Thirty years ago, the islands of Sumatra and Borneo were covered in rain forest, but human activity has reduced the rain forests significantly.

Deforestation

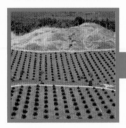

Large areas are cut down to make way for palm and coffee plantations.

Forest fires

"Slash and burn" fires are often lit on purpose to clear land for plantations.

Poaching

Hunters illegally sell animal parts like rhinoceros horns and elephant tusks.

Illegal logging

Trees are illegally cut down for wood and paper products.

TOTALLY TRUE - OR - FOOLISHLY FALSE?

A. When shopping for products containing palm oil, help the rain forest by making sure it's sustainably produced.

B. Products made from animals like tigers, elephants, and rhinoceroses make good presents.

C. Paper and wood products made from sustainable wood are the best kind to buy to help the rain forests.

Find the answers at the back of the book.

THE AMAZON

...the most famous rain
...orld. It's also home to
...es of indigenous people
...d in harmony with nature
...of years. The forest
...gen and water, which
...climate.

WHERE IN THE
WORLD?

Amazon
rain forest

SOUTH
AMERICA

AMAZON FACTS

Biome: Tropical rain forest
Area: More than 2.1 million
sq. mi. (5.5 million km2)
Rainfall: Between 5 and 10 ft.
(1.5–3 m) a year
Did you know?
13,700 species of plants
grow here and nowhere
else.

WHY DOES THE AMAZON MATTER?

 Trees store carbon dioxide as carbon, removing this greenhouse gas from the air.

 Trees produce oxygen that we breathe, and they release water into the air. This cools the climate.

 Plants and animals from the Amazon have been used to develop medicines.

THE MIGHTY AMAZON RIVER

The world's largest river, the Amazon, flows through the rain forest in the Amazon basin. The river is a key part of the biome, with at least 2,500 species of fish—as well as many mammals—depending on it.

Piranha

Giant otter

River dolphin

Capybara

ISLAND FORESTS

Islands are isolated pieces of land surrounded by water, so island forests are sometimes home to wildlife that appears nowhere else on Earth. When these habitats are damaged, entire ecosystems can be wiped out.

WHERE IN THE WORLD?

AUSTRALIA

NEW ZEALAND

MADAGASCAR

MADAGASCAR

Long ago, the island of Madagascar was part of a giant continent called Gondwana. By 88 million years ago, it had separated and become a beautiful, forested island. Many of its animals are endemic (only live there), including lemurs and the aye-aye. The aye-aye is an endangered primate with long fingers for pulling bugs out of trees. Humans have already wiped out its cousin, the giant aye-aye.

AUSTRALIA

When Gondwana split, a land mass broke away and eventually became Australia. Its forest animals include marsupials, most of which live nowhere else. Koalas are just one marsupial living in eucalyptus forests. Large parts of this habitat have been destroyed, putting more than 1,000 species at risk of extinction.

SAVING A SPECIES

Don't despair—we can turn things around! In 1980 there were just five black robins left in the Chatham Islands, near mainland New Zealand. Someone collected eggs from the last breeding female, named Old Blue, and gave them to foster parent birds. Old Blue laid more eggs, and her fostered offspring have brought the population to more than 300 birds.

TEMPERATE FORESTS

Temperate forests are at risk. More than half of Europe's endemic trees face extinction, and the U.S. has lost 90 percent of its natural forest since 1600. This puts animals in danger. Thankfully, some species are being brought back from the brink.

In Chinese forests, giant pandas eat bamboo. Every 10 to 100 years, all the bamboo in one area dies, so the pandas move to a new region. But large parts of their forests have been destroyed, so it is harder for them to find new sources of bamboo. There are fewer than 2,000 pandas left in the wild.

WELCOME BACK, GRAY WOLVES

Hundreds of years ago, gray wolves lived across large parts of North America, Europe, and Asia. They became extinct in many areas after humans hunted them and their forests were cut down. Wolves have since been bred in captivity and successfully reintroduced.

CRISIS FOR KAKAPOS

Kakapos are large, flightless parrots in New Zealand's temperate forests. Humans cut down trees and let cats, rats, and stoats loose. These predators ate eggs and chicks, and soon there were fewer than 70 birds. Now kakapos are protected, and by 2019 there were 213 birds.

LOVE TREES!

The trees that share your habitat matter just as much as the trees in rain forests. They help the climate, keep the air clean, support wildlife, and make you happy! Find out more about the trees around you.

WHAT YOU CAN DO

Trees in forests are often cut down for wood or paper. Forests are also cleared to make way for farming, particularly for cattle ranches and palm oil plantations.

✓ Eat a more plant-based diet.

✓ Check labels so that you buy only sustainable palm oil.

✓ Use both sides of a piece of paper when possible.

✓ When you buy new paper, make sure it's environmentally friendly.

✓ Reuse wrapping paper.

FACT
The world's forests suck up about 2.5 billion metric tons of carbon dioxide every year.

☼ BE INSPIRED! ☼
Professor Wangari Maathai (1940–2011) founded the Green Belt Movement (GBM) to plant trees in Kenya. Since 1977, the GBM has planted more than 51 million trees. Professor Maathai was awarded the Nobel Peace Prize in 2004.

AWESOME ACTIVITIES

Discover more about the trees that are helping
your habitat—and even add to their numbers!

PLANT A TREE

Plant a native tree—that
is a species of tree that
belongs in your habitat,
not one that has come
from another country.
Native trees
create the
best habitat
for wildlife.

HUG A TREE!

A tree's trunk gets wider and
thicker as it gets older. Hugging
a tree is a fun way to measure
how big it is. Measure the
distance of your arm span and
start hugging. You might need
some friends to help you hug
really old trees.

ARE YOU A FRIEND OF THE FOREST?

Test your knowledge . . .

1. Where would you
find a boreal forest?

A. Borneo

B. Russia

C. Madagascar

2. How many trees are
there in the world?

A. 3 million

B. 3 billion

C. 3 trillion

3. What is a kakapo?

A. A type of bird

B. A type of tropical fruit

C. A type of lemur

Find the answers at the back of the book.

GRASSLANDS

Grasslands grow where it's too dry for forests but where there is enough water to stop the land from turning to desert. These vast, mostly flat areas cover one-fourth of the world's land and contain a huge range of wildlife, even though there are few trees or other hiding places. Many animals, such as deer and antelope, gather in herds so they can work together to protect their families from predators.

TROPICAL GRASSLANDS

Tropical grasslands, such as the savanna in Africa, grow near the equator, where there are wet and dry seasons but the climate is warm all year.

TEMPERATE GRASSLANDS

Temperate grasslands grow away from the equator, where winds blow dry and strong, winters are cold, and summers are hot. In the United States, the prairie is home to the black-footed ferret, but only 370 are left in the wild. Only 1 percent of the original prairie still survives in the Great Plains.

NORTHERN GRASSLANDS

In the world's cooler north, temperate grasslands change with the seasons. At times, the landscape looks bleak, but it supports a large range of wildlife. Around the world, these grasslands are under threat from farming.

WHERE IN THE WORLD?

Prairies

NORTH AMERICA

ASIA

Steppe

PRAIRIES

The Great Plains in North America, also known as the prairies, cover 1.2 million sq. mi. (3 million km²). During the hot summer, grass seeds ripen and there is plenty of food. Some animals survive the winter snow and Arctic winds by hibernating.

Prairie dogs build underground burrows called towns. About 150 species of plants and animals depend on these towns. When farmers take over the habitat, prairie dogs are wiped out, along with the rest of their ecosystem.

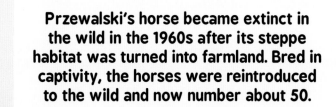

Przewalski's horse became extinct in the wild in the 1960s after its steppe habitat was turned into farmland. Bred in captivity, the horses were reintroduced to the wild and now number about 50.

THE STEPPE

The steppe in Central Asia covers 965,000 sq. mi. (2.5 million km^2) between boreal forest in the north and deserts in the south. Bleak winters are icy, but summers are scorchingly hot and dry. The steppe is home to many endangered animals, including the great bustard.

AFRICAN SAVANNA

The Serengeti's savanna in Africa benefits from a near-perfect mix of climate and soil, where grass grows well. This ecosystem supports the world's greatest numbers of hoofed animals, which graze on the grass, and a large number of big predators.

Giant herds of wildebeests, zebras, and antelope travel around the Serengeti, following seasonal rain. They make a circular journey of more than 620 mi. (1,000 km) to feed on the grass that grows after heavy rains.

SERENGETI FACTS

Biome: Tropical grassland
Area: 9,650 sq. mi. (25,000 km^2)
Rainfall: Up to 4.6 ft. (1.4 m) a year in the north
Did you know?
The Serengeti is home to Africa's largest ostrich population.

AWESOME ANIMALS AT RISK

The Serengeti ecosystem is at risk from poaching and climate change, which is drying the land. These are just four of its endangered species:

Black rhinoceros

Leopard

African elephant

Cheetah

TOTALLY TRUE - OR - FOOLISHLY FALSE?

A. Grass keeps growing even when an animal has nibbled it close to the soil.

B. Grass flowers need bees to pollinate them.

Find the answers at the back of the book.

SOUTH AMERICAN GRASSLANDS

There is a huge range of grassland ecosystems in South America, from the hot, rainy Llanos in the tropical north to the temperate Pampas in the south. Animals like the capybara and the Orinoco crocodile live in the Llanos, but their habitat is at risk from oil fields and farming.

WHERE IN THE WORLD?

Llanos

Cerrado

Pantanal

Pampas

SOUTH
AMERICA

In the 1800s, pampas deer were hunted for their skins, and at least 2 million of them were shot in just ten years. Since then, pampas deer have also lost 99 percent of their habitat.

VARIED GRASSLANDS

THE CERRADO

The Cerrado is the most biodiverse grassland in South America, but less than 3 percent of it is legally protected. The rest is rapidly being turned into farmland, which puts animals like the maned wolf at risk.

THE PANTANAL

The Paraguay River floods the Pantanal, creating the largest wetland in South America. But now it's also flooded with chemicals from farming and gold mining, which affect its wildlife, including the hyacinth macaw.

THE PAMPAS

Most of the Pampas grasslands grow in Uruguay and Argentina, but much of this precious habitat has been turned into farmland. Pampas animals are now at risk, including the greater rhea.

GO GREEN FOR GRASS!

The world's grasslands are under threat from pollution, climate change, and modern farming methods. Going green will help save grasslands for the future and for the plants and animals that need them.

WHAT YOU CAN DO

✓ Turn off lights when you are not in a room.

✓ Walk or bike instead of going by car.

✓ Organize car pools for trips that you have to take by car.

✓ Put on extra clothes when you are cold instead of turning the heat up.

✓ Turn off the faucet when you are brushing your teeth.

✓ Shower instead of taking a bath.

✓ Buy fresh food that comes from local farms.

¤ BE INSPIRED! ¤

David de Rothschild works hard to teach people about our precious habitats. His team made a boat from 12,500 old plastic bottles and sailed it across the Pacific Ocean. He named the boat *Plastiki,* and his voyage helped people learn more about plastic pollution.

AWESOME ACTIVITIES

If you can reduce the amount of water you use and the distance your food travels, you'll help reduce pollution.

TRACK FOOD MILES

"Food miles" refers to the distance food has traveled from where it was grown to your plate. Research some of the food in your kitchen and find out how far it has traveled to reach you.

WELCOME RAIN

Collect rainwater in barrels and use it to water plants. You can even channel water from your roof gutters into your container.

ARE YOU AS GREEN AS GRASS?

Test your knowledge . . .

1. Your laundry is wet. Should you . . .

A. Put it in the dryer for an hour?

B. Hang it up outside to dry?

C. Put it on and let it dry on your body?

2. What greenhouse gas do cows belch and fart as they digest their food?

A. Carbon dioxide

B. Oxygen

C. Methane

3. Which of these snacks is the cleanest, greenest choice?

A. Carrot sticks and a boiled egg

B. Potato chips and chocolate

C. Roast beef sandwich

Find the answers at the back of the book.

MARINE HABITATS

Seas and oceans form the world's marine environment. Water is where life first began, and it still teems with life, from microscopic plankton to the largest animal that has ever lived—the blue whale. Ocean water holds heat, making it a stable habitat, but it's always on the move. Water flows in giant currents, warming up near the equator and cooling near the poles.

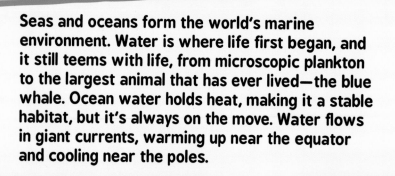

WEATHER MAKER

The oceans create the world's weather. As seawater absorbs heat, it evaporates into water vapor, forming vast clouds. Warm ocean air moves, creating winds that push the clouds onto land and bring rain.

OPEN OCEANS

Earth's oceans stretch across thousands of miles. From above, we see steel-blue water that rocks steadily in waves, and there are few signs of life. Beneath the surface, however, there are billions of animals swimming or floating through this massive habitat.

PREDATORS IN PERIL

Oceans are rich in food, so many large predators have evolved there. However, a quarter of whales and dolphins and more than 140 species of sharks and other large fish are now at risk, including . . .

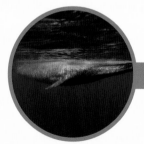

Blue whale　　　**Great white shark**　　　**Bluefin tuna**

OCEAN THREATS

The world's oceans and seas—and the animals that live in them—face a challenging future because of . . .

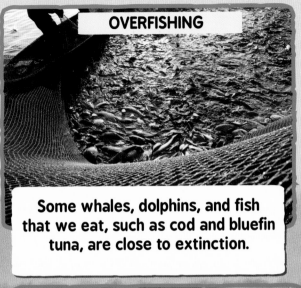

OVERFISHING

Some whales, dolphins, and fish that we eat, such as cod and bluefin tuna, are close to extinction.

CLIMATE CHANGE

As the oceans warm, they become more acidic. Some animals, such as coral, can't survive in such water.

POLLUTION

More than 80 percent of ocean pollution (including plastic, chemicals, and oil) comes from the land.

MASS MIGRATION

Animals swim across the oceans, helped by the currents, to reach their favorite places to mate, breed, and feed. Every year, gray whales migrate thousands of miles between icy Arctic waters and tropical waters near Mexico. By the time it's 45 years old, a gray whale will have swum the same distance as to the Moon and back!

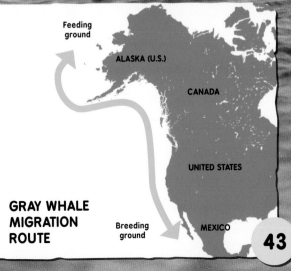

Feeding ground

ALASKA (U.S.)

CANADA

UNITED STATES

GRAY WHALE MIGRATION ROUTE

Breeding ground

MEXICO

43

COASTS

A coast is a habitat where the land meets the sea. Coasts change because waves batter the land, eroding it into beaches, cliffs, and rocky shores. Today 40 percent of people live near the coast, and that causes problems for these precious habitats.

DYNAMIC COASTS

A coast is a challenging place for animals to live because there are powerful waves, strong ocean winds, and tides. The tides make the sea level go up and down, so animals may find themselves beneath water at one time of the day and exposed to the air at another.

SUNLIGHT PASSES THROUGH SHALLOW WATER, SO ALGAE AND PLANTS CAN PHOTOSYNTHESIZE (CREATE FOOD)

WAVES ERODE THE COAST

THE SEA LEVEL GOES UP AND DOWN WITH THE TIDE

RIVERS EMPTY THEIR WATER INTO THE OCEAN AT THE COAST

MANGROVE SWAMPS

Mangrove trees grow in unique coastal wetlands, but many of these precious habitats are being turned into prawn farms. Half of all mangrove forests have been lost over the past 50 years.

The long-snouted seahorse is one of many coastal animals at risk from sewage, coastal tourism, and pollution. Chemicals from factories and farms are carried by rivers into the ocean.

CORAL REEFS

Coral reefs have been described as the ocean's rain forests because they're so biodiverse. Most of them grow in warm, tropical waters near the coast. Rocky reefs are built by small animals called polyps, and they depend on clean water to survive.

CORAL BLEACHING

At night, coral polyps stretch their tentacles out of their rocky cups to feed, and the reef bursts into color. Now many corals are turning white as their polyps die. The main cause is probably global warming, but plastic is also damaging.

FACT

In 2016 and 2017, half of the Great Barrier Reef's shallow-water corals died from bleaching.

WHERE IN THE WORLD?

The Great Barrier Reef

AUSTRALIA

THE GREAT BARRIER REEF

The Great Barrier Reef is a unique ecosystem that stretches for 1,430 mi. (2,300 km) along the coast of Australia. It's home to . . .

1,500+ species of fish

411 species of hard corals

134 species of sharks and rays

6 species of marine turtles

30+ species of marine mammals

ELEPHANT OF THE SEA

Dugongs are strange-looking mammals that grow up to 10 ft. (3 m) long. They graze on sea grasses in sheltered areas near coral reefs. Dugongs are protected in the Great Barrier Reef, but in other places they're losing their habitats as coral reefs die.

THE OCEAN FLOOR

Far below the sea's shimmering surface, there's a dark, silent place. The seabed is thick with mud and sand, and it's home to weird and wonderful animals. But even this distant place isn't safe from human activity.

SEABED SCOOPERS

Enormous boats called trawlers catch huge quantities of fish for us to eat. Their nets scoop up all the animals on the ocean floor, as well as the fish, destroying the entire habitat. Unwanted fish and animals are called bycatch, and they're thrown back overboard—dead.

ANGEL SHARKS

Angel sharks were once common in the Atlantic Ocean, but now they're critically endangered because they've been overfished. During the day, angel sharks rest on the sandy seabed near coasts, and at night they hunt.

Seaweed grows on rocky seabeds in shallow areas, where sunlight still reaches. It's used in some foods, such as ice cream, and in cosmetics. When seaweed is cut, many animals, such as seals, fish, sea urchins, seahorses, and starfish, lose their home.

TOTALLY TRUE - OR - FOOLISHLY FALSE?

A. The oceans are home to almost 500 different types of fish.

B. The oceans help control the planet's weather.

C. Many people rely on the ocean's fish as a source of food.

Find the answers at the back of the book.

THE GALAPAGOS ISLANDS

Famous for their unique wildlife, the Galapagos Islands are 19 islands and more than 40 smaller islets in the Pacific Ocean. Although this habitat is protected as the Galapagos National Park, it's still in danger from climate change and pollution.

WHERE IN THE WORLD?

SOUTH AMERICA

Galapagos Islands

SEA LIONS

Sea lions are hunted by killer whales and sharks, but their biggest threat comes from climate change. When the ocean gets too warm, the sea lions cannot find enough food to feed themselves and their pups.

MARINE IGUANA

The Galapagos Islands are home to the world's only marine lizard. The marine iguana basks in the sunshine and then dives into the water to feed on seaweed on the rocky ocean floor. It can stay underwater for 20 minutes at a time.

UNIQUE ANIMALS

Some unusual animals live on the Galapagos Islands, including . . .

Blue-footed booby

Giant tortoise

Galapagos racer snakes

RESPONSIBLE TOURISM

The Galapagos Islands are very popular with tourists—about 250,000 people visit this remote habitat every year. They're asked to be responsible tourists. That means following these tips:

Take only photos, leave only footprints.

Keep your distance from wildlife, and don't touch or feed wild animals.

Help clean up litter on the beach.

BATTLE PLASTIC!

Plastic pollution is turning our oceans into big, blue garbage dumps. We do need some plastic, but we can make sure that we use it responsibly. That means cutting it out of our lives whenever and wherever we can.

WHAT YOU CAN DO

Say no to plastic to reduce the amount that ends up in our oceans.

✓ Eat ice cream from a cone, not a plastic container.

✓ Buy fruits and vegetables loose, not wrapped in plastic.

✓ Refuse plastic straws. Your lips are perfect for drinking!

✓ Wet wipes contain plastic. Use a wet cloth for cleaning instead.

AWESOME ACTIVITIES

MAKE YOUR OWN SHAMPOO
Bars of shampoo don't need plastic bottles, and they also make great gifts!

PASS ON PLASTIC
Collect up any plastic toys you don't use anymore and give them to a thrift store or swap them with someone.

✖ BE INSPIRED! ✖
Help conservationists share information about the environment. **Ben Lecomte** swims enormous distances—such as 3,715 mi. (5,980 km) across the Atlantic Ocean—to raise awareness of ocean pollution. Find out more about his epic ocean swims at www.benlecomte.com.

ARE YOU A PLASTIC PEST OR A SEA SAVER?
Test your knowledge . . .

1. When you play sports do you . . .

A. Take a refillable water bottle?

B. Buy a bottle of water on the way?

C. Avoid running so you don't get thirsty?

2. What do you use to wrap your sandwiches?

A. Reusable cloths that are coated in beeswax.

B. Plastic wrap—it's so handy!

C. Nothing—grubby sandwiches are tastier.

3. You put your wet towel in a plastic bag. Do you . . .

A. Hang up the bag to dry so you can reuse it?

B. Throw the bag away?

C. Hide the bag and towel under your bed and forget about them?

Find the answers at the back of the book.

MOUNTAINS AND POLAR PLACES

Some animals and plants have adapted to survive in some of the most challenging habitats. The polar regions—the Arctic and Antarctic—experience extreme weather. Many mountains are exposed to icy winds and blizzards that cover the ground for months or even years at a time. Then in hot seasons, the sun scorches them with a burning intensity.

MELTING ECOSYSTEMS

Animals like the Alpine ibex have adapted to life in extreme conditions, but they're under threat. As ice melts, they have to find new places to live. Some will not survive.

FACT
The Antarctic holds 90 percent of Earth's ice. If it all melted, sea levels around the world would rise by 200 ft. (60 m).

MOUNTAINS

Life on high mountains has many challenges. Earth's thinner atmosphere at high altitude—great height—absorbs less of the Sun's harmful ultraviolet radiation. Mountaintops are often very dry, and the soil layer, if it even exists, is too shallow for tree roots to take hold.

WHERE IN THE WORLD?

CHINA

PAKISTAN   Himalayas

INDIA

THE HIMALAYAS

The Himalayan mountains include Mount Everest—the highest mountain in the world. Climate change is having a dramatic effect on the area. As ice melts, it affects the rivers and climate in the area, which will cause problems for the billions of people who live to the south.

ANIMALS AT RISK

Many mountain animals in the Himalayas are endangered, including . . .

Wild yak

Red panda

Siberian musk deer

At high altitudes, the air has less oxygen. Snow leopards have huge chests with big lungs to help them take in more air. They've been hunted for their beautiful spotted fur to the point that there are only about 3,000 left in the Himalayas.

TOTALLY
TRUE
- OR -
FOOLISHLY
FALSE?

A. Wild yaks use their horns to dig through snow and find plants to eat.

B. Red pandas are a type of bear, and they feed on bamboo.

C. Siberian musk deer are killed for their musk, a brown waxy secretion that's used to make perfume.

Find the answers at the back of the book.

THE ARCTIC AND ANTARCTICA

Global warming is a concern to people all over the world, but its impact on the Arctic, Antarctic, and tundra regions is especially worrying. These places are precious habitats for extraordinary wildlife, and they also help control Earth's climate and sea levels.

WHERE IN THE WORLD?

ARCTIC CIRCLE

ANTARCTICA

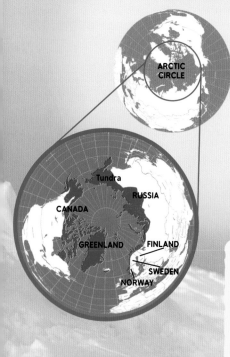

Tundra

RUSSIA

CANADA

GREENLAND   FINLAND

SWEDEN

NORWAY

Polar bears live in the Arctic—a frozen ocean in the north, surrounded by frozen land called tundra. The Antarctic is a continent at the world's South Pole. Both places endure long nights, short days, and freezing temperatures.

KEYSTONE KRILL
Tiny krill are a keystone species (they're the main food for many animals) in the Antarctic Ocean. In some areas numbers have fallen by up to 80 percent. If numbers fall further, other animals will starve.

CLIMATE CRISIS
As Earth warms, the planet's ice is melting. This has devastating consequences.

SEA ICE REFLECTS LIGHT BACK INTO SPACE, KEEPING EARTH COOL.

SUN

WHEN THE FROZEN GROUND MELTS, IT RELEASES GREENHOUSE GASES AND EARTH GETS HOTTER.

MELTED ICE CAUSES SEA LEVELS TO RISE AROUND THE WORLD. THIS RESULTS IN FLOODING IN COASTAL AREAS.

WHEN THE ICE MELTS, SUNLIGHT REACHES EVEN MORE OF THE OCEAN AND WARMS IT UP.

A GREENER FUTURE

Working together, humans can achieve incredible things. We know it's important to act quickly to reduce the damage we're doing to the natural world and its wildlife. You can decide what part you could play in creating a greener future.

Asian rhinoceroses in Nepal's Royal Chitwan National Park are protected by UNESCO—a global organization that preserves 213 natural habitats, such as the Mount Kenya National Park, where African elephants live. What similar local organizations could you help?

SCIENCE HOLDS THE ANSWERS

Science, technology, engineering, and math are key subjects to study for the future of the planet. We need to use science to understand the damage we're doing and to find the best solutions. Would you like to be involved in inventing new, nonplastic materials, monitoring gorilla populations in Ugandan rain forests, or designing greener airplanes?

✘ BE INSPIRED! ✘

Children and young people all over the world are campaigning to change the way we live. They hope to persuade politicians, companies, and ordinary people that the need to tackle climate change is real and urgent. You can join local and national campaigns to make your voice heard.

FIVE WAYS TO FIGHT FOR YOUR FUTURE!

Now you know the challenges that Earth faces, take action! Help for habitats begins at home.

✔ Join local nature groups that protect green habitats and wildlife near you.

✔ Reduce, recycle, and reuse things whenever possible to save energy and resources.

✔ Spread the word —lend this book to your friends!

✔ Find out more from conservation organizations such as the World Wildlife Fund, Conservation International, and Oceana.

✔ Write to your government representatives and sign online petitions, or ask an adult to.

GLOSSARY

ACID
A chemical substance, often dissolved in water, that can break down other materials or react with them.

ADAPTATION
The ability of animals to change their bodies and behavior to suit their environment. If something changes suddenly, they may not be able to adapt fast enough to survive.

ATMOSPHERE
A layer of gases around a planet, moon, or star, held in place by the force of gravity.

BIODIVERSITY
The range of animals and plants in a habitat. Some places have more biodiversity than others. In Borneo, 0.2 sq. mi. (0.5 km^2) of rain forest has more tree species than Europe and North America combined.

BIOME
All the animals and plants that live in a habitat, such as a forest, desert, or grassland.

CARBON DIOXIDE (CO$_2$)
A colorless, odorless gas released when fossil fuels such as coal, oil, and natural gas are burned. Volcanoes produce carbon dioxide, and animals and humans breathe it out.

CLIMATE
The average pattern of weather in a place over a long period of time.

CONTINENTS
Huge sections of land that move around on top of Earth's hot liquid interior. There are seven continents, most containing a collection of different countries: Africa, Antarctica, Asia, Australia, Europe, North America, and South America.

DEFORESTATION
The cutting down of many trees, reducing the size of a natural forest.

ECOSYSTEM
A community of animals and plants in one place, including nonliving things, such as water and soil. Removing one part of the ecosystem threatens the whole ecosystem.

ENDANGERED
A species of animal or plant that is in danger of going extinct (dying out forever).

ENDEMIC
A plant or animal found only in one place. Koalas, for example, are endemic to the forests of eastern Australia.

EQUATOR, THE
The imaginary line circling Earth's middle.

EXTINCT
A species of animal or plant that has completely died out.

FOSSIL FUEL
Oil, natural gas, or coal, which formed underground millions of years ago from decomposing plants and animals.

GREENHOUSE GAS
A gas such as carbon dioxide or methane that wraps around our planet, keeping it warm.

HABITAT
The natural home of an animal, plant, or other living thing.

KEYSTONE SPECIES
A species that an ecosystem needs in order to work properly. Prairie dogs are a keystone species because without them the whole ecosystem is badly damaged.

LIVESTOCK
Farm animals, such as cattle, chickens, and sheep.

MAMMAL
An animal that has hair or fur, gives birth to its young, and feeds it with milk.

METHANE
A powerful greenhouse gas produced when plant matter decomposes with no oxygen present. Natural gas is mostly methane.

OXYGEN
A colorless, odorless gas, mainly produced by plants. Animals and plants need oxygen to live.

PARTICULATE
A tiny bit of a material, often released into the air when the material is burned.

PHOTOSYNTHESIS
The chemical process by which plants turn sunlight, water, and carbon dioxide into food.

PREDATOR
An animal that hunts and kills other animals to eat.

PRIMATE
A type of mammal that has hands and forward-facing eyes. Gorillas, lemurs, monkeys, and humans are all types of primates.

REINTRODUCTION
When scientists put a species that has been lost from one area or habitat back into it and help them survive and breed.

SPECIES
A kind of living thing, such as African elephant or Bengal tiger. A member of one species cannot normally mate with a member of another species.

SUSTAINABLE
Food that is sustainable is gathered or grown in a way that makes sure it won't run out. That means keeping enough fish in the ocean to keep breeding so they can replace the ones that are caught.

TEMPERATE
Of or relating to regions with mild climates that lie between the tropics and the polar regions. Temperate areas often experience four seasons in a year.

TOXIC
Poisonous and likely to cause harm to plants or animals.

TROPICAL
Of or relating to the hot, wet regions surrounding the equator.

TUNDRA
The land south of the Arctic Circle, where the ground is permanently frozen.

ANSWERS

PAGE 11
HOME SWEET HOME: TOTALLY TRUE OR FOOLISHLY FALSE?
Statement A is true.

B is false: Palm oil plantations have replaced the forest homes of at least 193 animal species.

Statement C is false.

PAGE 21
FOREST HABITATS: TOTALLY TRUE OR FOOLISHLY FALSE?
Statement A is true.

Statement B is false.

Statement C is true.

PAGE 29
ARE YOU A FRIEND OF THE FOREST?
1B, 2C, 3A

PAGE 34
GRASSLANDS: TOTALLY TRUE OR FOOLISHLY FALSE?
Statement A is true.

B is false: Grass flowers are pollinated by wind.

PAGE 39
ARE YOU AS GREEN AS GRASS?
1B, 2C, 3A (3A has no plastic packaging, and it avoids meat from cattle. It's healthy, too.)

PAGE 49
MARINE HABITATS: TOTALLY TRUE OR FOOLISHLY FALSE?
Statement A is false: There are probably at least 20,000 species of fish in the oceans.

Statements B and C are true.

PAGE 53
ARE YOU A PLASTIC PEST OR A SEA SAVER?
Mostly (a): You are eco-friendly and a sea saver. Well done!

Mostly (b): Plastic pests use plastic and throw it away. Change your ways!

Mostly (c): You're doing a great job at saving your own energy, but you could try harder to save the planet!

PAGE 57
MOUNTAINS AND POLAR PLACES: TOTALLY TRUE OR FOOLISHLY FALSE?
Statement A is true.

Statement B is false: Red pandas are related to raccoons, not bears, but they do eat bamboo.

Statement C is true.

FIND OUT MORE

Check out **worldwildlife.org** to find out how the World Wildlife Fund is tackling climate change to protect our animals. See what Conservation International is doing for the planet at **conservation.org**, and look at **oceana.org** to see how Oceana helps protect the world's oceans.

Become a Climate Kid with NASA at **climatekids.nasa.gov**.

Explore your world with videos, fact sheets, and more at **kids.nationalgeographic.com**, and find out how to reduce, reuse, and recycle at **berecycled.org** and **wastebuster.co.uk**.